soft gold

soft gold

(danny francis)

L P P

library
partners
press

ISBN 978-1-61846-126-1

Illustrations by Danny Francis
Book and cover design by Celeste Holcomb

Produced and distributed by

Library Partners Press
ZSR Library
Wake Forest University
1834 Wake Forest Road
Winston-Salem, North Carolina 27106

www.librarypartnerspress.org

Manufactured in the United States of America

(also by danny)

you deserve flowers

(for)

anyone working
on being

braver,
sweeter,

softer.

lifting weights
at 5 a.m.

and

black coffee
with cinnamon

and
therapy over Zoom.

medicine

but what does healing
have to do with honey?

work.

work and
flowers.

said the bee

sometimes

when i think about

you,

i can feel
my teeth

filling
with

venom

and i remember how
much healing

i have left to

do.

angry.
sad.
anxious.
lonely.

allowed

that thing i shouldn't have said

(that you probably don't remember anyway)

and doing my taxes wrong

and dying alone.

up at night

and how
do you set down
the heavy thoughts?

only

as gently,
as gently

as you can.

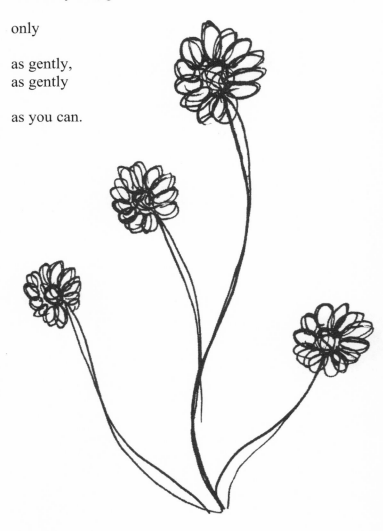

it wasn't perfect.

it wasn't everything.

it wasn't nothing.

sometimes

i want to reach out
and tell you how much

i miss the way you eat avocados.

she
loves
me.

she
loves
me
not.

you stepped on
my flowers

and i loved you for it.

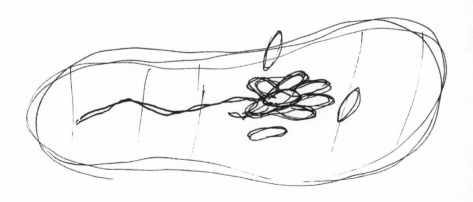

i worship rejection.

when i was little
i used to be afraid
of spiders.

now i think
i'm just afraid
of people.

maybe i'm a spider.

-arachno-agora-phobia

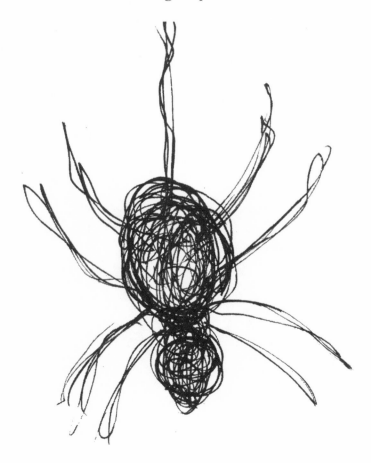

i wake up and work and go home.

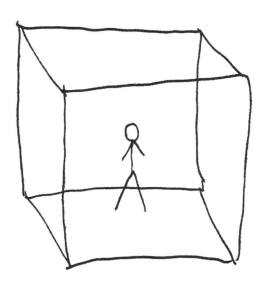

isolation

hold your loneliness

tenderly,

tenderly.

blue honey

i measure
time
in

matches

and
candles

and aches.

some mornings

i'm too afraid
to get out of bed.

i'll lay there for
hours and hours
buried under
my covers
terrified that if
i move even a little
then everything
will come
tumbling

down.

but god there are these
other mornings
when i wake up with
the bravest, softest,
most beautiful parts
of myself rising
from every pore
like a thousand soft
golden suns.

and i write poetry.

flowerbed

you can be
scared

and still be
brave

(and still be scared).

every

step
away
from
you
is
a
step
i take
towards

me.

walking away

i wish you healing

and muffins

and other soft things.

when waiting
didn't work
i started
filling in
the empty
spaces with

colors and
poems and

me.

groceries

2 red peppers

1 large onion

12oz canned pineapple

chicken

spinach

blue berries

gummy bears

milk

and flowers (for myself).

be your own lover.

dandelion

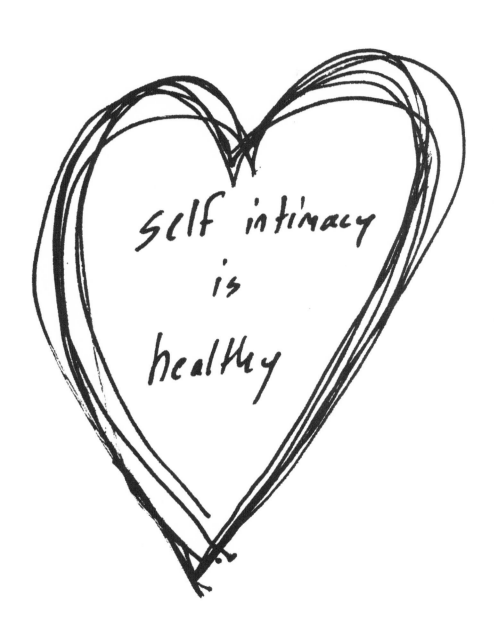

self intimacy
is
healthy

daisies on the
kitchen table
and alone
time

and tea mixed
with whisky

and some things
heal better
with a

spoonful
of gold.

manuka

i live and write
in teaspoons

(maybe i'm an ant).

if a seven-letter word like *courage*
feels like a scary place to begin

then try a six-letter word like *create,*
because creating is courageous.

creating draws us

in and
out of ourselves

conjuring brave
possibilities and
powers
during the times
when we feel
so impossibly

powerless.

and if you wanted to be a little more creative
then you could try a five-letter word like *quiet,*
because sometimes courage is that thing we do
quiet-ly.

like flowers quietly blooming in
your window sill

or

quiet whispered
words

like,

"i can do this"

"i can do this"
"i can do this"

whispered

when no one (but you)
is listening.

because whispered courage

is courage
is courage

is courage.

and if you need a word that's a little louder
then maybe try a four-letter word like *roar*,
because some parts of you deserve

your fullest voice.
your loudest voice.
your fullest voice.

your loudest roar.

and if you wanted a word to practice roaring,
then you could try three-letter word like *yes,*
because each time you say yes

you open a little

and live a little more

and a little more
and a little more

fully,
bravely,

fully.

each time.

and if you're not quite ready to say yes to yes,
then try uttering a two-letter word like *no*,
because saying no without fear

or shame
is brave work

and because

sometimes saying no
when we are afraid
can be even braver work.

and if you have to say no to no,
then practice a one-letter word like *i*.
practice saying it over and over again

like,

i
am enough,

i
am enough,

i
am enough.

sitting in this chair again,
fidgeting with my pen
while searching for

words,

sweet,
honest,

words

to help me untangle
all my fears of intimacy
and healing traumas
and lack of abs

and worth.

therapy again

talk about

sex
and
suicide
and
sharks

and other all the other things
you're afraid of.

lurking

talk about it

with ink

and honey.

i try to write about hard things
hoping that reading
might help you

soften.

in your way.

in your time.

some days

i don't give
a fuck about
growing flowers
or writing poetry
or healing

or honey.

and those days
are so important

too.

i feel loudly
and softly.

healing is

patience
and
desire
and
consistency
and

disruption.

there are parts of me that are

(still)

poisonous.

aposematic

i'm working on sweeter patterns.

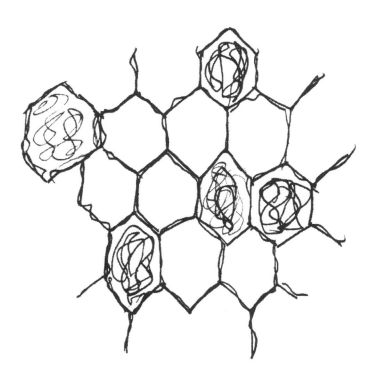

sketching flowers
at the laundromat

and the feeling of
clean sheets against
my skin

and
morning runs
and afternoon swims

and

lists
lists
lists
lists
lists

and compassion that patiently

grows like the moon

outside
my window.

tattoos
and
tangled hair
and
love
handles

and healing traumas

and other things
that

don't make you

less

loveable.

~~if you can~~
~~love me~~

~~then maybe~~

i can love myself.

water. sunshine.
rest. play.

space.

leg day

squats

goblet squats

lunges

bulgarian splits

curls

glute bridges

a walk with a friend.

and some days
a slice of pizza

heals best.

~~and~~
~~some days~~

it really is
enough
to just

be.

remember to breathe.

the work is hard

and
important

and

c o   nt   i   n   u o   u   s.

i'm not there yet,
but i will be.

yet but

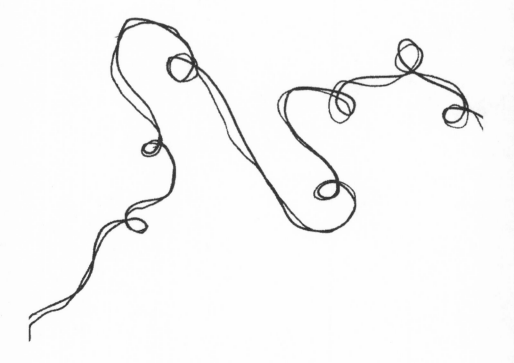

resilience
grows.

like

kind,
revealing words and
salted caramel ice cream
melting in a waffle cone
and the romance between
flowers and

bees.

soft magic

some mornings

i can feel
these

parts of
me

soft,
beautiful

parts of
me

edging closer

    and

        closer
        and
        closer

           and

           closer

             towards the sun.

i want to feel bravely, visible

again.

sunflower

self-abuse.
self-work.
self-care.
self-longing.
self-discovery.
self-intimacy.
self-boundaries.
self-love.

and flowers.

i love the way
you are learning
to love yourself.

i purred

(to myself).

i'm a messy bloomer.

i

apologize

if i've ever met
your genuine desire
to make a connection
with another human being

with suspicion or thorns
or one less drop
of kindness

than you

deserve.

listen.

you're going to
make mistakes

and that's okay.
it really is.

(i promise).

make mistakes.

talk about them.

learn about yourself.

boundaries
can be messy

and beautiful
and hard
and hard
and messy.

like
lovely
little lines,

scribbled,
and erased
and redrawn

around
and
around
yourself,

sketching

your ends
and
edges

with splattered ink.

drawing

expressing needs.
asking questions.
holding boundaries.

pillowtalk

two words,

i want,

spoken from your
own lips can make
the bravest sound.

i want to give you

words rolled
in sugar
and
warm hands

and tulips

and
the space

to bloom.

honeyflowersugarbaby

i want to kiss your magic

and your toes.

sunkissed

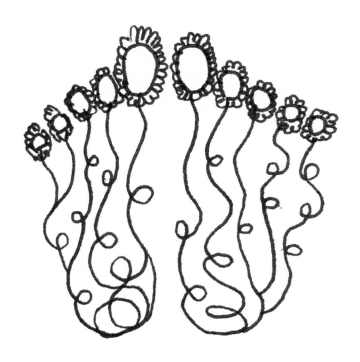

sharing fantasies
and traumas

and

remembering birthdays
and eye contact
and

post-orgasm farts

and other kinds of intimacy.

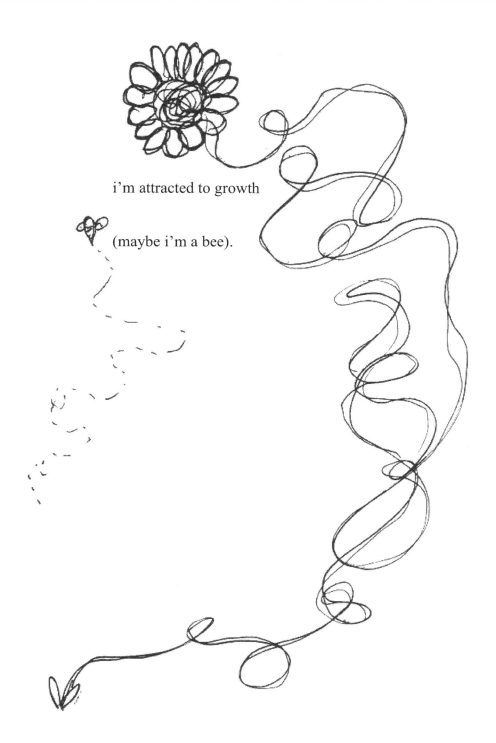

i'm attracted to growth

(maybe i'm a bee).

like

peanut butter
and
chocolate
or learning how
to love you
and me

at the same time.

so what if

instead of
me drowning in
you

or

you
drowning
in me

we just
went swimming

together.

skinny-dip-endence

blueberry pancakes
and lingering

nerves

and all the
sweet touches
from last
night

lingering
in my

skin

and syrup
in my beard.

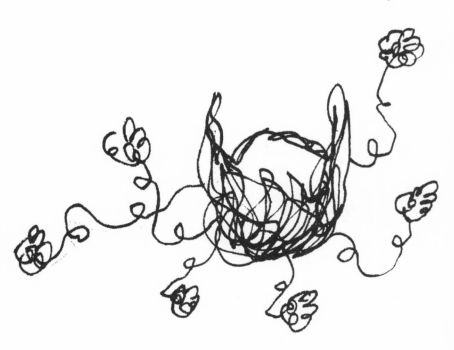

i'm all honey and
tangled flowers.

i use ink when
i'm afraid
(maybe i'm an octopus)

part of
learning
how to love
yourself is

the terror

that comes
from being
unable to hide
behind the
usual reasons

for why
you think
you are not

enough.

raw honey

the only courage
i've ever wanted
is the courage
to choose

myself.

and oh

what a beautiful risk.

(i hope these words find you
when you need to hear them most).

you are

so damn brave.
so damn brave.

you are resilience

and magic.

you are
a-walking-talking-gorgeous-damn-brave-mess

and a masterpiece.

you are
soft gold.

promise yourself

the moon

(big-self-love).

we really don't have time
to live any other way
than honest

(and kind).

daffodils and
armpit hair and
tenderness and
bellies and

other things that grow.

write a
love poem

(to yourself)

that ends
with these

words

(and i am enough).

i knew a sweeter kind of longing
when i learned that i could
love your garden,

but still needed to
grow my own

flowers.

a beard full of flowers,

earth brown eyes,

and a dirty mind.

sweet villain

i am a lot
and
i am enough.

sometimes when i get stuck i ask myself,
am i still doing the work?

because what i write is a reflection of
the deep relationship i'm working on
with myself every day.

it's not about writing something pretty or nice
in the same way a flower can be called

pretty or nice.

no. it's about work that is
courageous and messy,
irresistible and uncontainable
patient and resilient
in the same way a flower
can be called

blooming.

i love me.

i will make
a home
in these
kind bones

of mine.

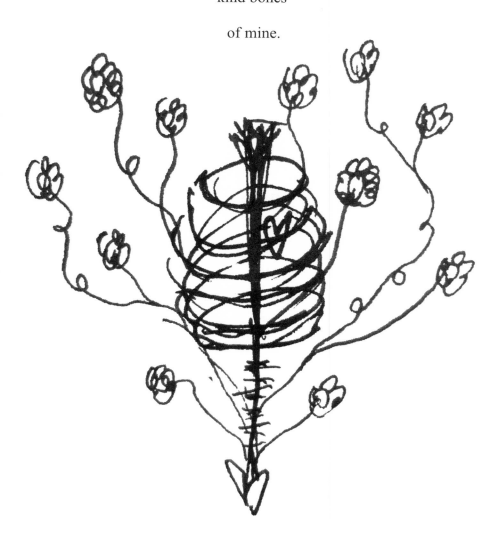

i will care for this
little life

and love her
as well

as i can.

mia

bloom,

you

ol' wildflower,

you.

dear heart

your

> feelings and
> thoughts and
> ideas and
> questions and
> answers and
> memories and
> stories and
> traumas and
> fantasies and
> longings and
> dreams and
> fears and
> wants and
> needs and
> groans and
> moans and
> sighs and
> songs and
> silence and
> doodles and
> drawings and
> ink and
> honey and
>
> poetry.

pour

and

all that
sweet stuff
that's been
growin

 in you,

that's for
you.
all for

you.

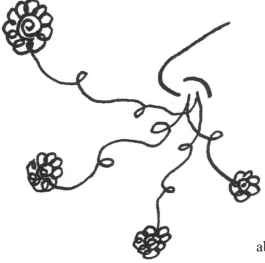

i really hope

that someday
soon someone
tells you
something

so pure

and beautiful
and funny
and true

about yourself

while you're
drinking

your morning
orange juice

that it makes
juice and
boogers

and flowers

shoot right out
of your

nose.

keep

softly,
fiercely

existing in

your own
sweet

ways.

and try to be patient.

there's honey
at the

end.

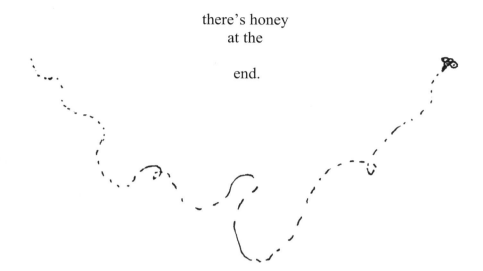

(acknowledgements)

i would like to say thank you to Library Partners Press for their continued support of my projects, my voice, and my ongoing work. i would also like to thank Jude Swanson for his friendship, honest insights and helpful edits. and a special thank you to all those who have reached out over the past year with comments and stories about how my words have touched and inspired them. your blooming inspires me everyday.

thank you for reading.

(about the author)

poet. wizard.
will buy you shoes.

danny is a recovery professional, theologian,
artist, and educator based in North Carolina.

this is his second collection of poetry.

(follow danny on instagram)

@theflowerbeardpoet

Made in the USA
Monee, IL
22 March 2022

93323549R00067